V.M. Fuentes

1

Trigger Warning

This poetry collection contains some sensitive
material but not limited to
racism, grief, gun violence,
and sexual assault.

Remember to practice self-care
before, during, or after reading.

Table of Contents

Passion's Reward

The cane trudged over floor, cementing yet another
streak that hounded him.

Barely making it to the chair nestled between
desk and bed.

Taking a moment to glance out
the window, remembering
greying clouds.

His fingers found their way
to a cracked keyboard
he'd had since college.

Click, clack,
Click, clack.

White walls shifted to a
world festering with
dragons
and
magik.

As the chapter neared its end,
an owl pecked the glass.

He met those familiar topaz eyes
saying,

"There's so much left to write…"

Yet, the room grew silent and

he noticed the husk.

Slumped over the keyboard,

his listless emerald eyes
gazed out the window.

A single "Hoo!" followed the
owl's ascent carrying
his spirit.

Back to his world,
Ankanowei.

Death's Mercy

Sheltered remains, hovering between consciousness
and purgatory
a flittering reminder of life's bitterness.

The sepulchre scorched white
suffers none to escape its iron
gates, yet flowers bloom outside

painting the cemetery in fields of
periwinkle blue and spring orchids.

When the reaper comes to
bury its dead and ferry
souls

that heart peeks out between
dusty rib bones but
its sloppy veins
and haggard breath
gushes clots onto
cracked stone.

Unperturbed, the hand of lush greenery
reaches through shadow and bone,
to grasp escaping heart.

Cradled in the last palm, the
heart felt soft grass and
warmth from the sun
sprinkling in.

Silence came as the heart beat

no more, yet even as the last
clot gushed forth

the heart saw those colors
once more.

Harkening to final days where
petals caressed its skin,
succumbing to a serene
fragrance
where bitterness left.

Fading memoir

A smile eclipsed bloody lips
marred by unspoken words.

Sheltering dreams in bone and
marrow that once strengthened
limbs to fly.

Now kindling, barely flinching as
scorched lungs leave you
breathless.

Pristine white cells, sworn to protect
harbor betrayal in its wake

Bereft of tears seclude sorrow
joining apathy or fateful fear.

Racing thoughts gasping to
finish another attempt — survive.

Hear a final hum and scribbling,
"Another falls…"

Flee! Shed mortal coil to fly
under cloud, among stars
to a place where dawn
and night
meet.

Hollow

The terrifying tragedy of losing one's love to vapid
abyss
where humor languishes over bones of nothing.

Opposing tempests feared such a gape,
if only to survive its toxic song.

Perilous and fortunate neither is,
rather
desolation riddles a soul.

That walking husk withers between
sentimental crowds of well-wishers.

If anything is left its buried
by
hopelessness, chasing memories
of loved ones gone.

Pictures remain but the sullen
eyes cry once more.

Hollow

Wayward

A world full of antique lizards
ruling dusty streets
on the hillside.

A barren wasteland of beauty, where
hawks stalk twilight skies

and roust in trees along
draconian ridges.

Scents of tumbleweeds and birch
linger deeper in.

Halfway through charred earth,
a neighboring vulture speaks.

Wayward snakes shiver in evening
gales amidst golden brush.

A wiser man would see eternity
in a flower, yet I stumble
across discarded leaves.

Towards a listless trail
where eyes hope for
a home beneath
twilit skies.

"You're just like your father!"

A phrase bound in torturous appraisal
reminding me of my fate.

Cursed to inscribe her words onto
shattered pieces of a
heart not worth beating.

"You're just like your father!"

Clamors to a rigorous shadow
as I walk in fear of women,
of whom I'm to become.

Beating bones bloody,
drowning screams in
Bible hymns

to escape the prison of
fate.

Harrowing thoughts
never relieve my
purpose

to regret my sexuality.
Does my sex frustrate you?

Am I even more perilous
grown into a black eyed
devil?

Tears caress my pillow

as I sleep alone,
surrounded by black.

How can I become more
if I was expected to
fail?

January 6th

Being seen doesn't mean you'll be heard
clothes can be shed, money can be earned,
but skin is constant.

On the heels of war, gunshots drown
voices of innocents lost
grievances left unanswered.

On the steps of DC,
injustice flourishes under
White Privilege.

Everyday, is a renewed ravishing
and raping of humanity,
stolen because it is "just"
and "necessary."

Fearful of another slave revolt
the unmasked KKK continue to
assail freedom,
limiting rights to breathe,
to walk, to be.

As they throw tantrums,
we lose rights.
As they conduct terrorism,
we lose lives.
As they storm DC,
we lose dreams.

They ready their guns,
their drums,

their young to
save America

while preparing for a
war to trample the rights
of us who remain in
their crosshairs.

their young to
save America

Allowance

History is written by the victors
with the blood of the
conquered.

Only scraps and whispers survive
our ancestors while
our history is
erased.

Since enslavement and genocide
the victors dispense
treasonous treaties and
laws.

Expecting gratefulness for
living in squalor, yet
with each decade
rebellion
occurs

and appeasement is ordered.

Tossing "Freedom" crumbs
on mangled earth,
inciting war between
black slaves
and
brown survivors.

the victors mock deaths
in streets, belittles babes
for attempting

assimilation.
Instruments of cruelty modified,

dignified from shackles to
cuffs,
from plantations to
prisons.

Yet, gratefulness to kneel
at their table is
expected.

Through burdens of law,
the victors scheme
to ensure the
illegality of skin.

Propagating their ever present
fears of us resuming
our place amidst
the carnage.

Wade through the blood,
incite pride lost,
to bellow,

"I am here!"

Educational Overhaul

American textbooks breed
compliance, casting
deceit into young
minds.

Submission born of
gratefulness is
instilled in
colored
bones.

Enslaved until reading
scraps, listening to
whispers.

Ancestors beckoning to
be heard.

Learn and heal battered
soul, drowning in
assimilation.

The connection of earth,
human, and beast
coexist in
peaceful
slumber.

Rekindle a spirit of
pride in traditions
and knowledge
forgotten.

Let communication
replace compliance,

Let compassion
replace cruelty,

Let generosity
replace avarice,

Let peace
replace war.

"True rebellion is
to live with a mind unfettered,
unshackled by their ways."

Gear your weapons,
a creative solace of
word or paint or tune.

Capture truth and dare to
hope for change.

Use pen to inscribe
wisdom
from ancestors.

Use brush to reveal
freedom
for all.

Use voice to enchant
healing
upon this land.

Late nights

speak to all but the worms,
even the birds consider
winds shifts
and tepid spells.

Worms feast, fuck, and
flee
burrowing deeper as
dawn strikes.

Bringing a lethargic sun
to stir the days flowers
and leaves.

Night comes on the
heels of stars
to gaze.

Owls reign, wolves
howl, but

Worms feast, fuck, and
flee
burrowing deeper as
dawn strikes.

Chalk

Harbors powdery futures,
lessons to be learned,
or lines drawn.

Never mistake a powdery
past for a
lackluster future.

Indeed, money tracks
the trade, a pittance
really.

When former blood once
crafted "0" before
conception.

Or surgical instruments
applied from head
to toe,

now sever futures
by white hands.

Still, chalk is here to
stay for can one
by more

when the past is
written in blood.

Whispers heard on
drunken nights

eclipse sleep.

Grieved Ones

Sometimes what's left of them is only the
Lies we tell ourselves.
Pithy laughter that pities the living
Yet, smile in remembrance.

They are the shadows at every eye corner
Whispers on the breeze.
And every nook and cranny
Where sanity is lost.

Pause at each phantom touch,
Feel their spirit pass.
And when you wake
In a dreamless state

See something left in doubt,
A lingering love or pout.

V.M. Fuentes

Loneliness*

I saw a man on a faded
park bench.

The air was torrid and
my wrists were bound.

My eyes grew wide as
he took out a sandwich
and thermos from his bag.

My nose wrinkled as
the smell of roast beef
with a crisp lettuce and provolone
between slices of rye bread
wafted up to my nostrils.

My mouth salivated as
he then unscrewed the
thermos to pour
hot coffee in his dented
cup. My ankles were bound.

As I passed by, he paid me
no mind as he watched

leaves flutter, heard the pigeons
cooing, and inhaled the flowers before
him.

Beneath a sky speckled
with clouds. My mouth was
bound.

Bittersweet Things

His tufts of bone white
hair crowned his

balding skull.

As my carriage ushered me
to a windowless prison
with a cot and toilet.

Devoid of even a mirror.
Instead, white walls.

Sometimes I think about
that man…enjoying the moment

as I have wasted mine.

*Original work published in The Dazed Starling:
Spring 2017

V.M. Fuentes

Raven Song*

Calling from the sky
its shadowy figure glides.

Heralding naught but
change in life's work.

Onslaught of humans
trembling before the call.

Charred feathers float
in front of stone,

beckoning — come.

*Original work published in The Dazed Starling:
Spring 2017

Somewhere Between*

a
tattered skirt and hallowed lies
is the abyss of
truth and sacrifice,

is nothing more than a patch
of hope and dreams now shredded.
Forevermore.

Silent all these years
with him still on me
and I don't care, but here I
stand, silent all these years.

Once ravaged I have returned from
the abyss only to re-stitch the
patch to another skirt,

to rebirth my dreams
never again tethered
to the memory of him who…

pinned me down, to tatter my
skirt
and muffle my voice, to shadow
my eyes fixated on the dark side of the moon,

the heaven where my screams have gone.

*First line revised, original work published in The
Dazed Starling: Spring 2017

V.M. Fuentes

The Broken*

Dawn breaks through
cracks in old blinds,

as clinking
bones slowly erupt.

The skeleton shuffles over
to its meat suit, taking

dull needle and twine,
stitches till it covers

rusty joints and marrow.
Soft thuds, it walks over

to an old wooden dresser
where it dips a finger

into a cup of blood
to paint a vibrant smile.

Next, it pops back two
eyes into hollow sockets

and with a roll, it gazes
to see itself with

eyes of amber and emerald.
A faint beating echoes

behind as it turns to
see what isn't decaying.

Bittersweet Things

It kneels to find slivers
and shards scattered

across the room. Yet
every attempt to

stitch, glue, forge, or
even freeze

together. Its heart
succumbs to an agony

which rents and eviscerates
again…again…again.

The mere memory of…well,
its heart glows momentarily

then scatters, for naught
will be the same as

it once was upon winter's
birth…

* Original work published in The Dazed Starling:
Spring 2018

Nocturne*

As night overcame day,
sun beckoned moon

to illuminate below
what stars could not

reach. Silky air tickled
leaves, petals, and webs

ss a sluggish drizzle
came. Often I wonder

from where this melody of
darkness arises. Yet

this question must elude,
for the lesson taught is

simplicity, not complexity.
As owl hoots in fellow

tree and crickets sing,
So I too enjoy the

rain.

* Original work published in The Dazed Starling:
Spring 2018

Nemesis

Soaring through kissed skies
its scarred chest and ruby feathers
track the breeze.

A cursory glance watches all
scouring craven rocks
and barren fields
for lunch.

The subtle tongue flick
beckons its descent.

Steadily gliding to meet
scaled foe, rattling
once again.

Fangs pierce air
just beneath its
talons as
it settles across the
field.

Wings arched out,
coaxing the snake.

Another tongue flick
tastes deceit
yet, it pounces,
shredding
armor.

The breeze carries its

victorious screech
past rocky craigs
before feasting.

Curiosity

Turning the key is a miserable child,
his toothy disposition, no more
unnatural than chilled apples.

Yet, a glaring candle summons
Wasps to coax the child's fumbling.

As the key broke,
all was lost to seizing shadows
and pickled fingers.

Hard Work

once helped us craft philosophy
and science, math and innovation,

cities and agriculture of global
envy was conquered.

Whipped and choked in
brown skins,
hard work makes the
best slaves.

Toiling the earth we
once mastered,
to serve white
means.

False freedoms written in
a misguided Constitution,
still shackles us.

Sterilized and imprisoned
to curb savagery, we
earn pennies on
the dollar

for work, hard work, suitable
for slaves.

Steal back ancestral pride to
make the work anew,
overcome prohibitions
with joyous laughter.

Testing

Crafted by white hands, ignoring the conquered
history of slaves and their progeny.

Administered to judge through a prejudicial Jesus
and stained education.

Intelligence is irreverently measured,
obscuring prevalence of cultural
slivers and beliefs.

Disbelief and prejudice marred the histories
only aliens built such cities and monuments.

Americans categorize and demonize
misunderstood survivors of
brown skin.

Appeasement is thrown in half
truths and rights, minor
victories

in a war to rediscover who
we were,
who were are.

Humans capable of valor,
truth, and justice.

Coming Home

There is nothing more terrifying than, "yes"
It begins anew, daily, yearly,
each time, I tremble at its sound.

Beholden to unkept promises
and eyes of loneliness.

"yes" is here, mocking the very
lips that birthed it, to feel freedom
among slaves.

Encumbered by the soul, "yes"
can only dole a just fate
to those unwilling to die.

"yes"
Growing up

"Tricky, icky,
mousy, wousy,"

goes the rhyme the angels
taught us.

Basking in heaven's glow
as they float beside me,
mumbling,

"Tricky, icky,
mousy, wousy,"

like razors digging into

34

my tongue.

Forbidding us to say anything
than,

"Tricky, icky,
mousy, wousy."

A haunting

They say, "the moon is a friend to the lonely."
Yet, its deafening silence are like screams
to mock me.

Inconsistent in its company, the moon wanes
stars blink as my eyes shut to his fingers
fumbling beneath my pants.

Before the sun breaks through, I
feel him slid free, climbing off,
staggering away to church bells.

Holier than thou, God's children,
go silent in the shadows of
the ivory steeple.

Can't break free soon enough

V.M. Fuentes

Something else

Poetry is neither rhyme nor meter
its something sweeter,
the infinitesimal words
of those refusing to die.

Or
just the psychedelic rendering of
an old man and a
boat.

Funny enough artists are
mistaken for people
half crazed, half special
even useless.

Yet, the dullard world
can't refuse their brushstrokes
and songs
or books of verse and rhyme
nor films and pictures
could be anything
less than.

Tend the invisible worlds
made discoverable
by a writer,

their legacy to time.

Perchance

The permissiveness and subtly of glass is forgotten by
most,
indeed, the commonplace of such reaps the benefit
of wealth.

Still, craftsmanship is minimalized by cheap
producers in lieu of centuries
of skill.

Sometimes nature graces us with brilliance,
lightning sears sand, scorches stone
of remembrance.

The fortunate favor ancient instruction to
avoid mistakes, yet times come and go
to show something of worth.

Alas, miniscule understanding of mud
tosses caution and severs wit.

Perchance

Meaning

Sometimes what's left of us is
nothing more than
memories forgotten.

A dying flicker of
speech left to those
who finally left
a name.

Yet,

the appetizing delights of the world
are no more distracting than
those on the straight and narrow.

Can meaning truly be found
in divining the
mysteries of
beyond?

Suppose there's nothing
more to say or do
except,

Live!

We Can Be Better

There are few civilizations who have known peace,
buried and conquered their voices lay
in blood-stained dirt.

Centuries away whispers vanish and elude,
for what is humanity but violent?

Tattered cares and wayward stares mark
history's ledger.

Full of meaningless quotes, cyclical wars,
and cursed screams.

Sure, some of us have known silence in a
turbulent world.

But few are so detached to let
this world fall away.

Come, learn forgiveness in strife, humility in
avarice, love in apathy.

Bend your ears to talk and mouths to listen,
if not, we'll never learn to dance.

Are we so blind to understand that love
encompasses rainbows
and skin?

The day has come to reverse laws
that enslave and discriminate.

Yield to healing hands gifting
food and water
to the next generation.

Bestowing the burden of struggle
to build upon dreams
of freedom
and
peace.

Rest, ancestors, rest,
it is our turn to
change the
world.

Dizzying Daydreams

Hours feel like minutes and moments
like weeks,

just a blur of words seamlessly
threaded in hazardous waste.

Where are the ones who dream?
Building empires from dust
and
medicine from air.

Erase the criticisms of today
for life is not without
this joyous affair.

Establish the impossible
to tackle the improbable
and
leave the possible
to others.

Strive to comprehend whispers
and the incoherent
nature of music.

There lies a magic beyond
the soul to cure,
to heal,
to listen.

V.M. Fuentes

Zoom Class

Drunken eyes gleam over the screen,
you could swear by it.

Wasted effort trying to capitalize on
exhausted subjects who

consume streams of humorous
nonsense for sanity.

Engage in the momentary buzzing
and disconnection

where frustration blooms
and anxiety yields.

Yet, it's a haven for those
unreachable in the
classroom.

Giving breathing room
to lessen social pressures
and awkwardness.

A screen to temper
interactions, freeing
encumbered minds.

Ode to teachers

It's the teacher that torpedoes the spirit
nary a chance of revival.

Students rife with tears and depression,
falter at their keyboards,
attempting to finish
another
assignment.

An instrument, a scalpel that further
deteriorates minds, young
and old.

Or they can cultivate another chance at
success.

Sleepless hours and zoomed out eyes,
teachers wake, choking down exhaustion
and frustration.

Again, they sit, trying to breathe and smile,
instructing the next generation
to keep step with the times.

Necessary guides
in a world of tyranny and
prejudice,

teaching us
to hope amidst
despair.

V.M. Fuentes

The Packhorse

Working day in and
day out,
nights at school
days at work.

It wasn't until the
Packhorse said,
"I love you."

did I realize it was
my mother.

What meager portions
could be paid to
erase the debt of life?

A mother's love is
worth more than
a mere "thank you"
can surmise.

Persona Non Grata

"They're bringing drugs. They're bringing crime.
They're rapists."

"Chinese Virus! Kung Flu!"

"Redskins, ignorant savages!"

"Go back to your country!"

Stars and Stripes conceal atrocities
as the stench of crimson mud
and desecrated bones

are ground into brick and
mortar for a White House.

The Constitution has long been the Master's whip
to ensure our compliance.

Even though
we speak their language
and follow their laws,
to avoid bullets
and a rope.

We have died in the Trail of Tears,
Detention Centers, Internment Camps,

by lynch mobs and badged conquers.

Terrorizing us, erasing us

as the media twists
headlines,
reminding us of our place.

Yet, our skin reveals a
flame
beckoning us
to gather as one.

Charged by laws mocking
our existence,

we continue
to march
under a hail
of bullets.

Inscribe the message of
our ancestors
on your
souls,

"You are not free because
a law says so, you are
free because you
are human."

We continue to bury
our dead before
marching,
announcing
to the White House,

"We are Human!"

Life's Masquerade

"Be yourself (but not like that)."

am I so weird to deserve a label?

The world has little use for those breaking

the mold.

Still, I break my cheeks, trim my ears to believe

in a fool's normality.

I paint my face soulless with eyes weeping

for a soul, compromised.

To learn the healing trick of

staying me cannot

come sooner.

Before I say, "Farewell"

my ears shudder to hear,

"You are worth it."

Only then will this mask be

Forgotten.

V.M. Fuentes

"From my cold dead hands."

Banners and chants uphold this creed
as corpses litter school hallways
and classrooms.

Up and down the streets they parade,
sexing the gun fetish all
require to
subvert a survivor's cries.

"Compliance over communication" is the NRA motto
or is it "Shoot first."

Words can coax cold steel from warring hands,
if only we can offer a chance.

Descalation is key to survival and disarmament
even more so.

Ah to be the generation that smelts
gunmetal into a memorial
to the dead.

Instead of bullet bouquets and
festering tombstones,

a hail of rain to bloom
orchids and fruit.

Thunder echoes hallow laughter
in halls of justice
if only we can find a way to relieve
the gunman's itch.

Secrets you'll never know

buried in marrow and tattooed on veins
they live to sacrifice my being.

I was once drunk on power over life
yet, the dreading reality of
blood leaves me
speechless.

Perhaps the skittering shadow I call
my own is less demonic.

A specialty to resent caring for children
and siblings tricks my frown
to smile.

Past the graveyard where I buried my
sex, it calls to me in
shameful intimacy.

A hallway of portraits trail my
history of woe
concealed in harmless
smiles.

The suicide I survived on pills
as my iPhone wailed in
anticipation.

Bottled up disbelief gathered from
loving mouths when
I said, "I was raped."

Now, harken to understand the
petulant smile of those
away.

If you dare listen to a story
or two,
beware the truth in lies

for you cannot handle
my blistering cackle

as I regale how
my shadow consoled
me in deepest
agony.

We walk among you
all smiles and
frowns

weaving through crowds,
seeking a place
to laugh
in forgetful remembrance.

To be kind is a breath
of fresh air among
a world that
forgot to say,

"Hello"

It's okay to be a Man...

You were not born cursed
to war, rape, or
abuse.

Yet, choice separates man from
beast.

Tarry a moment to consider
the ripples of those
actions.

If not, one yields to assumptions and
follows the mold.

Pitiful is the man too consumed by
fear of another's potential
only genocide
remains.

Or demolish generational burden
of misogyny to prevent carnage.

Accept the role of compassion
and teaching to
violence
and rage.

You are more than tradition
and silence.

Cry and admit healing for
wounds long buried

beneath a machismo
mask.

Emotion doesn't disqualify
manhood
nor does identifying
as male.

The daunting task of
living honorably
can inspire
self-hatred and shame.

Still, breathe the air to
renew strength
and
walk among brothers.

Consent

isn't as tricky as most believe.

Rather than shattering a soul
one asks to glimpse
beneath the
veil

"Pleasure shouldn't be tempered
by a 'yes' or 'no'"

Yet, agency over one's body is priceless.
and
belief of the event soothes
irreplaceable wounds

Consent

isn't a card to play, but an innate right.

Revoked whenever, sometimes
forever

The power of words shall
remain contained

in "yes" or "no"

only a monster fails to
understand this

"Your Body, Your Choice"

labels

husband, wife, student,

worker, child, bastard,

victim, schizo, dog,

straight, black, other,

it.

they anchor us to categories

of infuriating simplicity.

fracture our selfs to

be invisible or upgraded

to 3/5s.

are we not more than a designation

to avoid confusion?

being human is more than existence,

illegality, and strife.

be careful trying to fit inside a

checkbox, you may find yourself

lost in a world of

stunning realities.

travesties, really,

how can many compete

in a box?

humanity changes with

the seasons.

if stagnation were the game

we'd have remained

groping in the dark.

About the Author

V.M. Fuentes recently published his fourth poetry collection: Bittersweet Things to express some liberal political poetry. Currently, he has published three poetry collections: A Corpse Parade, We're Still Here, and A Greying Horizon. In his early twenties, he acquired a BA in Creative Writing and an MA in Forensic Psychology to enhance his creative prowess and understanding of human nature. While working on his doctorate, V.M. Fuentes is querying his first fantasy novel filled with arcane spells and fantastical creatures. When not delving into his magical world, V.M. Fuentes enjoys reading, drinking too much tea, and spending an absurd amount of time on his laptop.

Twitter: @VFue5
Instagram: vm_fuentes
Website: www.vmfuentes.com